Foreword

Anchor Books is a small press, established in 1992, with the aim of promoting readable poetry to as wide an audience as possible.

The poems in *Anchor Poets From The South* represent a cross-section of style and content.

These poems are written by young and old alike, united in their passion for writing poetry.

I trust this selection will delight and please the authors from *The South* and all those who enjoy reading poetry.

Andrew Head
Editor

ANCHOR BOOKS

POETS FROM THE SOUTH

First published in Great Britain in 1995 by
ANCHOR BOOKS
1-2 Wainman Road, Woodston,
Peterborough, PE2 7BU

All Rights Reserved

Copyright Contributors 1995

SB ISBN 1 85930 087 1

CONTENTS

1914 - 1918 - 199 . . .	G M Thorn	1
Places	Leslie E Thomas	2
Dorset - God's Acre	Julie Whale	4
Delayed Outside Bournemouth	J P B Shepherd	5
Around My Dorset Village	Rosemary Shaw	6
Southern Sun	Hilda Stewart	7
And We Forget	Ruth Panton	8
Tyneham	Devina Symes	9
Go Hug A Tree	May Strike	10
Sherborne Abbey	John Pryer	11
West Stafford	Frederick E Mold	12
A Gift In Your Hand	Lorraine Thompson	13
Margaret Marsh	Catherine Franco	14
On Chesil Beach	Jennifer Ackerman	15
Rushton Village Church	Janet Poulsen	16
The Dorset Man	E Chaffey	17
Dorset Place Names	Olive Scott	18
Weymouth, The Place Where I Was Born	Silvia Noakes	19
Portland	E V Paddock	20
Tolpuddle Whist	J Littlewood	21
Dorset, My Home	Wendy Edwardson	22
The Isle Of Portland	R B Thomson	23
Bridport In Dorset	F H G Fuller	24
In Memory Of Daddy	Ann Tilt	25
Untitled	Thomas C Ryemarsh	26
Aeroplane	L P Buckland	28
Darkness	L J E Farley	29
Ichlesham	Dilly Dillon-Guy	30
Shackles Of Age	Sue Paine	31
Why?	J A Roberts	32
Spring	Christine Spurrell	34
Hampshire	Joan Lambert	35
Nightfall	Alasdair Aston	36
Short Of Time	Nicky Dicken-Fuller	37
Ode To Basingstoke	Robert J Lambert	38

Ordinance Survey Sheet 186	A G Willis	39
The Solent	Chris Dixon	40
Winchester Cathedral	M Rowland	41
Twyford Down	Mark Weeks	42
Time	Joanne James	44
Southampton Is The Capital Of France	Patrick Art Cooper-Duffy	45
The Christmas Spirit	Susan Gamble	46
Pride Of Lace	Grace Graham	47
Wishing On Constellations	Suzanne Stratful	48
Eager Beavers	D W Johnson	49
At Granny's House	Gehanne Erian	50
The Night Of The Storm	Lotte Wakeham	51
Poem For Julia	Simon Taylor	52
A True Friend	Sarah Maycock	53
Godmersham Park	M Wilson	54
The Bluebells Are Growing	Gerald Roberts	55
The Beacon	Judy Bugg	56
Life On The Wight	A D Beaumont	57
St Helens Shore	Beverley Beck	58
Early Call	Philip Cook	59
Sandown	Paula Jacobs	60
Across The Water	Linsey Brown	61
Woodside Bay	Mary Grace Jones	62
Perseverance	Albert Hart	63
On The Cliffs Of St Lawrence	Chantelle Terry	64
Our Great Wight Hope	Edward Lyon	65
Our Fun Island	Frances M Rapley	66
Alone Again	Kim A'Court	68
All's Not Rosy In The Garden Isle	Maureen Matthews	69
Our Garden Isle	E Maxfield	70
Trip To The Needles 1994	Julia Perren	71
There Is An Island	Lawrence Holofcener	72
Island Refuge	Barry Jones	73
Portrait Of An Isle	A L Dowden and L T I Dowden	74
By The Sea	Liz Pecksen	75

The Isle Of Wight	Joyce Shotter	76
Time On Your Hands	June Lane	77
Yaverland	C West	78
Home	Chris Pennell	79
The Haven	Jane Elgar	80
My Island	Sam Lea	81
Ventnor In Spring	Ivy Barnes	82
A Tribute To The Arch Rock	Will A Tilyard	83
St Catherine's Down	T C Hudson	84
My Heaven	Lois Prior	85
The Longstone	Nigel Cantelo	86
Ode To 2 Miscarried Children	Derek Barretto	87
The View Of A Hillingdon Housewife	Wendy Edwards	88
The Heart Of London	Eve Schmidt	89
Non Old London	Lewis Breakspear	90
Young Clergy On Retreat	Mark Oakley	91
War And Peace In The Nineties	Leah Carpenter	92
The High Horse Has A Rider Still	Mary Frances Mooney	93
I Learn To Speak	Charlette de Christi	94
London 1995	Sheila Atherton	95
London	Doris Sherman	96
London, Much Maligned	Peggy Trott	97
Golders Hill Park	Miriam Elissa	98
Time On My Hands	Shirley D Press	99
Poem On The London Underground	Jean Beith	100
London	Marjorie W Bedford	101
In Loving Memory Of A Cat	Hilda Jones	102
Bad News	C Holmes	103
Untitled	John Spiller	104
Grade 1 Listed Building	E Hyder	105

The Blue And White Bridge	Pauline Long	106
Foreign Glass	Graham Hagger	107
Tell Me The Truth About London	David A H Clark	108
The Enigma Of London	B S Ashwell	109
The Sea	Margaret Brown	110
Restoration Of Westbury White Horse	Rosemary Smith	111
Flowers For You	Carol Shaikh	112
Birthdays	Margaret Brown	113
Eternal Spring	D E Porter	114
Behind The Hedges	Brokers Wood	115
On Marlborough Downs	Kay Boorman	116

1914 - 1918 - 199 . . .

A cobby little man
With old, milky eyes,
Achieves a sprightly hobble,
And tells me how he journeyed back
to the old battlefield,
and saw memorials to a hundred thousand men,
dozens known to him,
Hampshire men,
Alton men.
And in his mind how he still sees
Craters, big as towns,
Where men and horses fell,
And drowned, unwounded,
in the mud.
He 'stopped one' in the second battle of the Somme -
Patched up,
Sent back to 'Eepers',
he survived.
So few - just a handful - did,
and he was one.
His eyes are watering from looking back
Down those long years.
But he feels better, having gone,
'It's settled something in my mind',
he says,
'and I can sleep of nights'.

G M Thorn

PLACES

Derbyshire and Lanarkshire
And little Lower Swanick,
These are places on the map
Where people all take tonic.

Apuldram and Beckingham
And valiant Buckler's Hard,
These are places on the map
Where people all sweep the yard.

Punnett's Town and Twyford Down
And fabled famous Norwich,
These are places on the map
Where people all eat porridge.

Westward Ho! and Felixstowe,
Not forgetting old East Ham,
These are places on the map
Where people all eat cold spam.

Tandragee and fair Tralee
And Pompey in its prime,
These are places on the map
Where people all waste the time.

North and South, and Neath and Louth,
And loitering leafy Kent,
These are places on the map
Where people all pay the rent.

Smuggler's View and Tenby too
And Royal Tunbridge Wells,
These are places on the map
Where people all hear church bells.

'Urban Scream!' and 'Village Dream'
And hamlets far from fame -
These are places on the map
Where people all live the same.

Leslie E Thomas

DORSET - GOD'S ACRE

God was sitting in His Heaven,
A broad smile upon His face,
He'd just been very busy,
Creating a wonderful place.

He had filled it full of beauty,
With bright colours, rich and rare.
Much thought had caused its landscape,
And now none of the land was bare.

It was full of teeming riches,
Its creatures fashioned with care,
All in harmony living,
With the people He had put there.

Its people were true and honest,
Firmly rooted in the soil,
Loving, caring, and sharing,
Going about their daily toil.

They all loved this place as He did,
Wide open spaces and hills,
The woods and shady valleys,
The clear flowing rivers and rills.

He had filled the sea with fishes,
And put birds into the air.
The coastline He'd created
With no other could He compare.

By now God was more than rested.
He felt like taking a stroll.
Along He walked to His acre,
To Dorset - the best place of all.

Julie Whale

DELAYED OUTSIDE BOURNEMOUTH

Just so -
the train is late again,
sitting in some godforsaken suburb
in the rain,
waiting for who knows what.

The train is always late -
they never let it go
but make it wait
to meet the tardy coaches
of some other broken-down
and stranded train.

I'm tired of waiting.

I'm late in getting home -
all day the rush
of silly city life has left me
short of temper.

Now the rain
will make us later once again
and I will have to bear the strain
of sitting quietly here
annoyed and tense,
hating each moment
in the filthy train.

J P B Shepherd

AROUND MY DORSET VILLAGE

Like sentinels from former times
Round barrows mark the Ridgeway lines:

On ancient lynchets, stark and steep,
Browse polka-dots of cows and sheep:

And dry-stone walls of tumbled blocks
Are testament to earlier flocks:

The bubbling springs from chalkland Downs
Fill wells and winter bournes in towns:

On distant hills are monoliths
In circles of strange hierogliphs:

Small hamlets built by peoples' past
Reveal themselves as bumps in grass:

White cliffs are 'ceding to the seas
As they have done through centuries.

What monuments will still hold sway
To show that we have passed this way?

Rosemary Shaw

SOUTHERN SUN

From my window
   What do I see,
Rooftops, Chimney Pots
   the odd tree,
Blackbirds, Thrush
   and Seagulls nesting.
Hills in the distance
   on which colours are resting
Blues, Pinks, Orange
   and Reds
The birds are settling
   in their beds,
Down, down, down
   sinks the sun
The beautiful colours
   merge into one,
Darkness is here
   The Curtains are drawn
The sun has set
   until the morn.

Hilda Stewart

AND WE FORGET

She's remembering
As she lies there
Oh what was once the marital bed,
The sheets still soft, worn,
Scented by now absent lover
Unwashed and comforting,
At least to her,

There's no bucking up
No pulling herself together
She's fixed in memory
Times goes by
But she pays no attention.

And when I called to see her
She made no attempt to hide it
The cup from which I drank
Was rinsed
Not clean
Someone else's sugar in the bottom
And though to me the tea was sweet
I knew she had tasted sweeter.

They say love makes you do crazy things
But I say the fear of losing it, makes you do worse
And when it's gone
Its the fear of forgetting
And never feeling it again
Yes, I must admit
Love is strange.

Ruth Panton

TYNEHAM

There's a village in Dorset called Tyneham,
It's nestled in the lovely Purbeck Isle,
Search for the locals you'll never find them,
Except in the graveyard, where they rest awhile.

Barnes, Wrixon, Driscoll, Grant,
Gould, Wellman and Everett,
Minterne Knight, Cleall, Bond,
All carved in stone lest we forget.

Miller, Chilcott, Styles and Cooper,
Richards, Stickland, Taylor, Frend,
Freeman, Ridout, Toms and Ellis,
Faithful souls until their end.

Sacred to the memory of Tyneham,
A quiet prayer I offer today,
To all those generations who lived here,
Until evacuation day..

Devina Symes

GO HUG A TREE

If people would only relax, they would see,
What a wonderful world it can be,
But they're rushing here and rushing there,
With hardly a moment in their lives to spare.

I sit here watching them as they go
With nothing in their lives to show.
Like little ants they never stop
Running around till they're fit to drop

Why don't they stop and look at the trees,
And see what a great healer mother nature can be.
So I beg of you sir, as I watch you go by.
Why don't you give my suggestion a try.

Smell the sweet flowers and the woods after
The rain, and then maybe your life, would not
Bring you such pain.

Go a little slower and just say hello
And then on your face, all the joy it will show.

Don't walk by me with that frown on your face
Please Sir don't be in such haste,
Please Sir just try it for me
Go on, go hug a tree.

May Strike

SHERBORNE ABBEY

When first to Sherborne Aldhelm came
There was no Abbey, School or town;
This saintly man, with heart aflame
With faith and love, was not cast-down;
But cheerfully he moved among
The heathen peasants in this place
In minstrel's garb, and with sweet song
Won o'er their hearts, by God's good grace.

Where Aldhelm's harp with ringing sound
Attracted folk in Saxon days,
The Abbey rose. 'Tis hallowed ground
From centuries of prayer and praise.
Beneath this vault of lace-like stone
Gregorian Plain song once would soar.
With Benedictines' mellow tone
These panelled arches ring no more.

We may not right the ancient wrong
Inflicted by a Tudor King;
But Eucharist and Evensong
Still render praise. The townsfolk sing,
The organ peals; the golden thread
Of music, down the years,
Binds us to them, the long-past dead.
This lifts our hearts; we lose our fears.

John Pryer

WEST STAFFORD

Just round the corner from the church,
Low roof and open door,
With space to park a dozen cars
And squeeze in several more,
We're welcomed by 'The Wise Man',
Our friendly village pub,
With beers and wines and spirits
And all they call 'pub-grub'.

Just round the corner from that inn,
High roof and oaken door,
With pews to seat two hundred
As in the days of yore,
There beckons us the Parish church,
Our medieval shrine,
Which offers every Sunday
A wafer dipped in wine.

Lord, ere we leave this corner,
Our low roof or our high,
Our treasure, gentle Dorset,
Its vales, its coast, its sky,
Reveal to us your presence
And our neighbour's need;
Give to us compassion -
To care, to share, to feed.

Frederick E Mold

A GIFT IN YOUR HAND

Beauty, History, Freedom, Peace,
Hills, Buildings, Air, on lease.
Privacy, Solitude, acres of land.
Such a golden gift all in your hand.

Tucked in a village that's one and for all,
With bushes, hedgerows and avenues tall.
Rivers, streams, that run so deep,
Feeling safe at night when you go to sleep.

Places of interest, motorways few,
Living in the countryside, my dream come true.
Travelled the world, there's nowhere to match,
My home in Dorset was the perfect catch.

Lorraine Thompson

MARGARET MARSH

The wind was blowin' rather harsh
When I met my old friend - Margaret Marsh.
We thought we'd go for a meal and tea
In a restaurant - far too Plush for me.
The Charlton Mackrell was all a - Shrivel
And so I ordered the Curry Rivall
Said she 'this dish is too 'ot to aundle
And the light 'tis only a Bishop's Caundle'
I watched her lick the platter clean
Then I saw her face turn Enmore green
I had a port and she a brandy,
Lucky I had Sixpenny Handley
Then under a Charlton Horethorne tree
We sat and drank ten cups of tea.
She doesn't Wareham, I's got me pride,
So I'll be off to Piddletrenthide.

Catherine Franco

ON CHESIL BEACH

Wild, grey seas, pounding, tearing,
Lashed to fury by raging gales,
Huge white horses, rearing, bucking,
Foaming manes, streaming tails.
Beach of pebbles, scraping, grating,
Mauled and teased by mighty sea
Adds its theme of ceaseless sucking
To this crazy symphony.
Mountainous waves, pummelling, thundering
Spew their evil flotsam ashore:
Dead bloated cow, stinking, rotting,
Weed, lines, floats and boxes galore.
Two gulls above, wheeling, screeching,
Black, racing clouds, heavy with rain:
Scenes like this, magical, deafening,
Inspire and refresh, again and again.

Jennifer Ackerman

RUSHTON VILLAGE CHURCH

What a busy little place
It is on a Sunday morning
Once the service starts
The vicar speaks
The organ plays
The people pray
The worst of the week is forgotten
And forgiven and laid to rest
In the village church
The wine is drunk and bread is eaten
We give the church a penny or two
During the week the flowers get watered
And the brass gets cleaned
In the village church

Janet Poulsen

THE DORSET MAN

I was Dorset born and raised,
And I don't care who knows it.
I don't like the city life,
And when I'm there I shows it
I like it where the winds blow free,
And the stars shine clear from above.
I don't like those city lights,
Its the country life I love.
Born down in Dorset where the trees grow tall,
And the grass is green where nature's been
And men like me feel small.
And down in Dorset where the air is clean,
The fields of brown, all around,
Turn different shades of green,
There's rolling hills and daffodils,
And lambs that jump for joy.
There's gentle rain and peaceful lanes,
And the love of girls and boys.
I love the country and here I'm going to stay,
And when I die I hope to lie,
In a quiet Dorset grave.

E Chaffey

DORSET PLACE NAMES

We first came down to Dorset so many years ago,
Then - only on a journey on our way to Westward Ho;
We passed a lot of funny names - like Piddle towns and Puddles -
And wondered if our maps were wrong? Or we were in a muddle?
But soon we sped right through these parts and on our way to Devon -
Our journey's end for holiday in a County named like Heaven.

Those Dorset names I thought about while we were still in Devon
For soon we would be leaving there - our holiday sounding Heaven;
Then back through Dorset's country lanes with funny sounding places?
With sea-shore near, and fine clean air, this county still embraces.

Now ten years on we've settled down, quite happily in Dorset,
We took our time to make the move, with no one round to force us!
How pleased we are we took the route we found with funny names -
For now on journey's round about, we play the place name games;

There's Affles and Puddles and Winterbornes too,
And Tolpuddle Martyrs to name just a few,
But one Dorset saying that is always ahead -
Those odd Dorset names are there to be read!

Olive Scott

WEYMOUTH, THE PLACE WHERE I WAS BORN

The dignified Georgian terraces sweeping round the bay
Watch unmoved as little speedboats dance amid the spray.
The safe silver sandy beach dazzles under summer skies
And the familiar voice of Mr Punch mingles with a seagull's cries.
Holidaymakers by the score compete for places in the sun
And with buckets and spades and ice-creams children enter the sea at a run.
At little old shops in narrow streets sunburned visitors stop to buy
Outrageous picture postcards displayed outside to catch the eye.
In the quaint but busy harbour guarded by Nothe Fort,
The lifeboat's at her mooring and the ferry's leaving port.
The crabbers unload their catch delaying traffic on the quay
And there's a salty taste upon the lips as the wind blows off the sea.
And when winter comes, all visitors gone, the skies steel grey and bleak,
The cold east wind blows through the town with a haunting piercing shriek
And the beach festooned with seaweed is disfigured damp and raw
As the sea no longer gentle, pounds the unresisting shore.
I stroll the empty promenade, hotels closed, deserted shops, all forlorn
Yet rejoice that Weymouth's my home town, the place where I was born.

Silvia Noakes

PORTLAND

It rises steeply from the sea,
Very stark and bare
The colours mostly grey and white
A tree! It's very rare

The winds they blow so strongly
Full of salt and spray,
The grass is very short and brown,
Along the cliff top way.

It is a cold bleak island
Right out in the sea,
The home of many sea birds, there
So wild and oh! So free.

I wandered along the pathways
The wind it blew my hair,
A sense of peace and freedom came
From those grey rocks so bare.

E V Paddock

TOLPUDDLE WHIST

Whist night, Monday, at seven thirty
Ladies Jean, Joan, Win and dear Bertie
Welcome folk from near and far
Cliff and Iris come by car
There are prizes for all to see
Chocolates, cakes and a box fo tea
'Hearts are Trumps', we hear Ben call
Down here at our old village hall.

Pat and Jean have smiling faces
Trumped my Queen, King and my Aces
Losers move to the next table
Pleased to see my partner Mable
Time to chat and have a break
Biscuits, tea and coffee to make
Sugar, one or two I ask Peter?
Hurry! Quick! 50p for the meter.

'Spades are Trumps' Ben calls again
My score is low the same old refrain!
Is it luck or is it skill?
Should have stayed at home and watched The Bill
Lillian looks across at me
Oh! She's won that box of tea.
Failed again! Booby! I'm such a flop
Goodness, Gracious! I've won the lollipop!

Goodnight Gladys, Brian, Irene and one and all
Come and join us on *Mondays, seven-thirty*
at our *old village hall.*

J Littlewood

DORSET, MY HOME

Our beautiful unspoilt county,
No motorway here is in sight,
But quiet picturesque villages,
A haven of peaceful delight.
Magnificent stretches of shoreline,
Our heritage closely preserved,
Enchanting, this county of Dorset,
A title so justly deserved.
Our history seeps from all corners,
It leaves some remarkable tales,
Many ships have set sail from our harbours,
Many travellers have wandered our vales.
Our wonderful county of Dorset,
What more could a land have to give?
Although I have thought about travel,
It's Dorset that I'll always live!

Wendy Edwardson

THE ISLE OF PORTLAND

Portland so rugged and so bare
The Lighthouse stands so majestically there,
Portland the isle we love
Reaches to Heaven thro' the blue sky above.
With its heart made of stone
In a circle of sea,
The wind and the rain
Play a soft melody,
While it watches *Weymouth*,
Far over the sea.

R B Thompson

BRIDPORT IN DORSET

A beautiful coastal scenic view
Between Dorchester and Lyme
Is the town of Bridport
That's hardly changed with time

It's mentioned in the Doomsday Book
The Black Death claimed its toll
It gave its men to two World Wars
Etched on the Honours roll

It's famous for its nets and ropes
In countries far and wide
For fishing and in times of war
Their needs have been supplied

There's hamlets nestling 'tween the hills
And churches to inspire
Do visit us from time to time
In beautiful Dorsetshire

F H G Fuller

IN MEMORY OF DADDY

He who left this world today
loved and appreciated the
English countryside.
He always welcomed Spring with joy
And knew where the finest bluebells and primroses grew.

He who left this world today
loved to garden
His fingers green grew the finest roses
I've ever seen
And his sweetpeas were a dream.

He who left this world today
Loved animals both wild and tame
Especially dogs
whose friend he was
Sandy, Suki and little Bob.

Ann Tilt

UNTITLED

All is quiet
But for the lone bird,
Singing his last song
Of the day.
But, who is listening?
The sun has long since
Left the sky,
Leaving a trail of tints
Pale rose and yellow,
Like a watercolour artist
Painting the landscape;
Mist slowly fills
The hollows in the field,
And the moon
Is gaining strength
But, who is watching?
Perhaps most of us
Have forgotten how;
We need a market price
To guide us,
No faith
In what is free;
You, who stand
Staring into space,
Say you find faith
In moments
Such as this:
Dare we interrupt
To ask -
How, when and where?

Simple is the answer
And simple is the way - Be calm, be quiet,
Listen and look,
Faith will come,
Proving its value
Higher than any
        Coin of Realm.

Thomas C Ryemarsh

AEROPLANE

They tell me the plane is a wonderful thing
Flying through the air like a bird on the wing
Up through the crowds to the sky so blue
I think what they tell me isn't quite true

We've worked all year and now for a break
I'm trying to look happy but it's all a big fake
Cases packed with clothes and towels
And in the hand luggage a cork for the bowels

We arrive at the Airport all smiles and laughter
No turning back now it's me they're after
Through passport control the holiday begins
First stop the bar for a couple of large gins

We are on the plane and ready to go
Oh how I wish that I had said 'No'
Down the runway and up in the sky we soar
Now my breakfast is over the person next door

Up in the clouds trying to look brave
I undo my seat belt and then do it up again
Sitting there nonchalant with a big grin
I think I'll have another very large gin.

We are nearly there the airport's in sight
I couldn't care less I'm getting a bit tight
We descend to the earth like a giant hawk
I wonder what the hell happened to that cork!

L P Buckland

DARKNESS

13.36 says the clock,
And I know that must be wrong,
Because it's dark.
But without you here
My whole life is dark
And I have lost all sense of time.

You are miles and miles away,
But despite this, although our bodies are apart,
We are together
In Mind, Spirit and Soul

L J E Farley

ICHLESHAM

An ancient church the village boasts
An skyline mill and pointed oasts.
While orchards, hills and valleys blend
With gentle sheep the shepherds tend.
A haven of tranquillity
Set down in Sussex . . . fair to see,
For although traffic passes through
It never seems to spoil the view.

In the old inn atop the lane
Quaint relics of the past remain.
Farm implements adorn the walls,
A warm hello the landlord calls.
Step in the garden and espy
The medieval town of Rye
And, way beyond, the majesty
Of Folkestone rising from the sea.

The folk who in the village dwell
Play their part in the scene as well,
Give strangers greetings with a smile
And spare the time to talk awhile.
If some good cause should on them call
They hold sales in the village hall,
And happy children I have found
Play in the recreation ground.

In Autumn orchards are alive
With merry laughter . . . those who strive
To gather the last apple in
Know well the farmer's praise they'll win.
Each passing moment thanks I give
That destiny ordained I'd live
Here, in the very home of grace.
May time preserve this charming place.

Dilly Dillon-Guy

SHACKLES OF AGE

There they all sit in their twilight years
Their bodies giving up that wilful fight
Sitting alone in their own little worlds
Are they happy we will never know.

Some are happy to just sit and smile at you
Some do nothing but moan
Some are so sweet they seem untrue
But together they are all at home.

It seems so sad to get so old.
When the body your mind is trapped in,
Leaves you out in the cold.

The memories, still there
of when you were young,
Running and jumping,
Playing in the sun.

What a terrible way
to spend each day.
Being tortured by who you were,
When you were young.

Sue Paine

WHY?

Everyone's against me
Calling me names
Spreading false rumours
Let me end it all.

> Why don't they leave me
> Pick on someone else
> Leave me alone
> I hate you all.

I'll do it this time
I will you know
I'm not joking
Not this time.

> That's it . . . one . . . two . . .
> Cut it deeper
> Three, four, five
> Almost there now.

That's it . . . I've done it
What a mess
I've done it, I have
I meant it . . . see.

> But what did I gain
> It's all over now
> Nothing but blood
> I've got what I wanted.

I've cut too deep
I can't turn back
Now it's the end
Is there no hope.

I could have talked
Sorted it out
But I was too hasty
Help . . . don't let me die.

J A Roberts

SPRING

Spring is here there's nothing to fear,
Winter has gone the snow's disappeared
Out comes the crocus and daffodil too
Even the primrose say's 'Hello' to you.

The Sun is shining the sky is blue
The rabbits are running bees are humming
Look over the fields, what do you see
The lambs they are playing like you and me.

The blackbird up high building his nest
He's very busy just like the rest
Singing their songs while they work away
No time to stop no time to play.

The fox and his cubs play in the warm sun
Spring is here and new life has begun.
So don't be downhearted you just have to smile
Because Spring is here for only a while.

Christine Spurrell

HAMPSHIRE

Your leafy lanes and golden beaches call me;
Your ardent rivers, flowing to the Sea.
The speckled trout, in crystal waters gliding -
The mayflies waltzing one brief, hurried spree.
The leafy Downs, where Chalkhill - Blues are dancing,
The golden haze, the poppies' scarlet blaze;
The skylark's joyful singing, high above me,
The smell of grass on glorious Summer days . . .

Joan Lambert

NIGHTFALL

Round the neglected darkness of your mind
In odd corners lie
A forgotten collar, rusty shoes, old hoes.
You haven't been here for twenty years or more.
Was it a death or madness broke it off -
The haysel and the ploughing ?
You listen to slow voices in the gloom.
A heavy horse stands steaming in the yard.
Dogs sit about to catch unwanted scraps
And lamps are lit as labourers disperse.
The ceremony stills. It must be soon
The breathing finished in an upstairs room,
The lamps went out for ever and your plough
Rusted to the state it lies in now.

Alasdair Aston

SHORT OF TIME

It's five o'clock in the morning. The alarm starts to bleep.
I wish that I were somewhere else and could go back to sleep.
But it's time to make the breakfast. It's time to walk the dog,
And then commute to London in the early morning fog.

Am I in time for the conference? My mind begins to race.
Dash from train to escalator. Why do I keep this pace?
The tube train's by the platform. It's packed right to the door.
Is there time for me to board it? Is there room for just one more?

I glance down at my briefcase. Do I have my notes to read?
Are they at home, in the study? Have I all I'm going to need?
Should I try to be pro-active? Should I dominate and guide?
Perhaps to be re-active would produce a smoother ride.

My paper now delivered, I don't have time to eat.
I hail a throbbing taxi, waiting eager in the street.
It threads its way to Waterloo. Will I arrive on time?
When is the next train due in, if I am too late for mine?

Seats are already taken, but at least I caught the train;
I stand in stuffy corridor and let it *take the strain.*
Sitting now inside my car, I join a traffic jam.
Wanting so much to be back home: how frustrated I am!

A warm welcome awaits me, with licks and wagging tail,
Anticipating tasty tea and then a forest trail.
Kettle on; the dog is fed; flashing light takes my eye:
The answerphone reminds me that I should not pass it by.

Requests by post and answerphone; the telephone now rings;
E-mail arrives; the printer runs and new demands it brings:
Work to be done that will not wait; it must be done tonight.
I sit down at my keyboard and the VDU so bright.
Communication's easy in this nineties life of mine.
But twenty-four hours in a day - I am so short of time!

Nicky Dicken-Fuller

ODE TO BASINGSTOKE

In the chill of this December night
Darkness is wearing its blackest cloak,
And yet, ahead, I see a welcome sight,
The bright, inviting lights of Basingstoke.

To outsiders, it's known as Doughnut City,
Due to its wealth of roundabouts,
And no-one could really call it pretty,
With its concrete towers and lager-louts.

Most people regard the town as a joke
When they read about it in a book,
And yet, if they visited Basingstoke,
They would surely return for a second look.

There's a concert hall, cinemas, an ice-rink too,
Night clubs and discos with neon lights,
There is just so much to see and do,
It's the place to be on Saturday nights.

Robert J Lambert

ORDNANCE SURVEY SHEET 186

Learn the symbol, crack the colour code
For orchard, tow path, church with spire
Pointing the way to bridle path once deep in mire
An ancient greenway, then a drover's road
Leading to Alton market. There sheep and cattle fed
Where now a bypass road is marked in red.

In this map so carefully surveyed
Read the climate, habitat and histories
In its scientific facts and mysteries.
Beneath the red and orange lines of major road and byway
There are straight streets of Roman highway
Small trees clothing valley, scarp and hollow
Then closer contours reaching up to tumuli and barrow
Viking names, boasting of Alfred, Saxon Tuns
King John's Hill where huge caparisoned horses heaved
Wearily pulling iron shod guns
And tired men made camp among the leaves.

The language of a map must speak in metaphors
For marked paths may not be rights of way
Pheasants lord it over man on nettled nests
Guns scatter death on Sunday afternoons
In Farringdon and Chawton.
But, passport for my journey on my knee
Climbing Selbourne Hanger is not difficult for me
Rough wind and weather doesn't matter
Nor the varied seasons play their tricks
On my Ordnance Survey sheet 186.

A G Willis

THE SOLENT

With white sails set against a ribbon sea,
she airs her Jewels for those who wait.
Then sweeping surf from pebbled shores at Lee,
in silence funnels quickly through the strait.

She hears the clang of rigging at the mast,
the rattle sound of stones upon the beach.
Gripping, groping hulls of Tankers as they pass
and tripping surfers in the Hill Head reach.

Then changing, She, without a warning sign,
from playful calm to violent slashing riot,
Striking unsuspecting yachtsman from the line
and swiftly back to unrepentant quiet.

Chris Dixon

WINCHESTER CATHEDRAL

Arches of stone like branches of trees
Hold massive pillars with greatest of ease
Lacy iron gates, worn wooden doors.
Shadowy corners, cold stone floors
Shafts of gold sunshine, through old glass windows
Saints in their chapels, with feet on their pillows
Sweet singing of choirs, loud peeling of bells
Such magical treasures in our heart dwells
It is here, we seek comfort and courage anew.
A wonderful place for the many or few
May its strength and comfort never decrease
To give love, with its beauty, and hope of sweet peace.

M Rowland

TWYFORD DOWN

We drive daily through the cutting.
Dusty workmen stare through fences
defiantly. Uniformed guards pace,
the crackle of radios like cow bells,
boots white with chalk, slowly pace.

Scree like icebergs, great mounds
of hillside, piles of rock, rise
about the tiny men. Canyons
screwed into the land around
smoke like a dragon's throat.

A phenomenal maggot, the carving
gnaws the Down, sinking underground.
Green escarpments open like lips,
and from the ashes a screech
of heavy machinery swells the air.

We used to visit the tufted hill
that spills this drool of excavation
across the valley. Strands of river
kept us from the city. Strands of hair
wrapped your face in the warm breeze.

Steel mesh almost reaches where we sat.
Twined to its wire are harlequin ribbons,
and tinfoil leaves, wavering. Five ragged trees
stand as if petrified by a gale; each
a ragged traveller in its seat.

Barely inscrutable, guards gather inside
the line, puffed in attention, eyes upon
the silent tribe as the crunch and shuffle
of policemen breaks; a flurry of outrage;
twisted arms, and legs are dragged away.

Ten minutes and over, hauled over
the hill to waiting vans. The thin line
thins to an eruption of engines;
sword-toothed cats grinding the raw slope.
The leaning trees lean a little further.

Mark Weeks

TIME

Time is the most important thing
It ticks away and what does it bring
Joy for some, misery for others
Lost is love between sisters and brothers.
Time does not stand still when a clock stops
Forgetting the time opportunity drops,
There is always time to make amends
Then you will find who are true friends,
If time runs out it can be too late
To put back the pieces, this is fate.
What useful purpose for those who waste time
A withering thought and such a crime
Make the most of this precious stage
The time is yours to act your age.
Children will follow what adults do
Listen and learn it is all up to you.
When time marches on try to look back
Just for a second for something you lack,
In the whole of my seventy one years
Half was spent in laughter and tears.

Joanne James

SOUTHAMPTON IS THE CAPITAL OF FRANCE

I was told by a poet of Soton light,
Balmy as though it was France,
On reflection he could be right,
As tourists mill over flowers
And poets swoon over Bargate.

I have seen that French flair for fashion,
Transformed to Hampshire punk
Of Hippy musical style
Playing cupid with a bottle of wine.
With two lovers and a dog on string,

I hear the sounds of the bus and cars,
The clash and shudder of the traffic
Beating a retreat in the late afternoon
I remember all it's not what it seems
And Southampton is the capital of France.

Oh, Southampton city of lovers,
With romance on every street,
I bow before your majesty.
The rainbow colours are your natural hue,
And all that has been said before is untrue,
Southampton I love you.

Patrick Art Cooper-Duffy

THE CHRISTMAS SPIRIT

We buy the January bargains
To save us extra cash;
We re-cycle all the paper,
That others think is trash,
We have all these great bargains,
None of which they will not like;
We groan and struggle home with them,
'Wish I'd have used the bike'.
The carol singers; all out of tune, wanting
money, for their mums;
But no-one really likes them; we wish they wouldn't come.
It's money money money, it gets dearer every year;
We eat so much food that it makes us feel quite queer,
I wish the indigestion tablets, and fizzy remedies
they would dish out,
To heal our poor sick stomachs and hangovers too no doubt;
I'm allergic to the season
But people will always say,
You should have the Christmas spirit, be bright, cheerful and gay,
I now don't ever bother, to open up my Xmas gifts,
As it's only the same as last year *usually some aftershave that whiffs*
So goodbye dear old Christmas,
Only another twelve more months to wait;
And if I don't have another upset stomach
Then Christmas will be great.

Susan Gamble

PRIDE OF LACE

What magic was my sister's intent darting her small steel wand with fanatical velocity
Was it a spell printed in black on white? Bespectacled scanning reassured correctness in mentally recording progress
The mystery grew in length and agitatedly my curiosity, perhaps a present for a small fidgety sister
I regarded the busy fingers with fascinated awe and ventured to ask the purpose of such industry.
'It's pretty' I ventured 'who is it for?' An answer curt and busy 'You must wait and see' and lo I did see and receive
Such fine lace to adorn my cotton panties, to bedeck that useful garment my plain derriere wrap
How I loved my lacy drawers, they were the ultimate in serrated edged luxury lingerie trimming
Angles of feminine adornment peeped coyly from the hem of my gingham dress, I was the envy of all females.
Sorrow was mine when wash day chores claimed my pride in the interest of hygiene for the weekly wash.
Then the joy of reunion when cleaned ironed and snowy white they were returned to my loving care.
Disaster came wearing them to school I found my cherished ones drooping below uniform level.
Teacher was emphatic with her reprimand Tidiness was next to Godliness in the pursuit of academic attainment.
Humility complete when the snapping of elastic cascaded my laced cotton and nestled on my skinny ankles.

Grace Graham

WISHING ON CONSTELLATIONS

Dream on Libra for that spangled jewel
Of freedom and justice - like some ingenuous fool!
Could Pegasus not canter across while
Orion unsheathes his sword: cuts the trial
And tribulation of man? Could Andromeda
Cyclone all ills away: spin crying far?
Star-gazing, mesmerised by beauty - world's horror
Dimmed by such radiance: hopes for tomorrow
Like peace - an interstellar miracle.
Piscean end to famine: full belly, full smile.
'Oh, Venus, descend the sky, Morning Star;
Did a comet fling from its tail: plague Aids?
Could seven Sisters kiss that better Pleides?

Suzanne Stratful

EAGER BEAVERS

On the hill. I stood quite still, and listened to the night.
Little sounds came drifting in, from beneath the starlit sky.
A busy world that comes to life. While men to quietly lie.
The rustling in the undergrowth, the grunts, the clicks, the sighs.
The owls hoot, and the foxes cry.
I have also stood atop that hill, when the sun was in the sky.
Then the sounds I heard, were far different from the night.
Eager beaver bustling man. A roaring rushing sight.
It would do them good, to stand upon that hill, and listen to the night.

D W Johnson

AT GRANNY'S HOUSE

White door bell like a beaming moon,
The same bone yellow knife handle and spoon,
The smell of lamb in cider and potatoes hot,
The bubbling sound of peas in the pot;
Woman's Weekly piled up neat,
Sherry trifle served up as a sweet;
Dutch doll in cabinet and ornate egg green,
And music boxes collected from places she's seen;
Sweet Swiss tune floats from the box,
Honeysuckle, raspberries and pink hollyhocks;
Happy Families, with Mrs. Rabbit and Miss Fox,
And chocolate crackelets and cakes and the tick of the clocks.

Gehanne Erian

THE NIGHT OF THE STORM

Getting darker, darker.
Suddenly, Fzzzzz!
Plunges us into darkness,
Crash!

Thunder roaring, lightning zig-zags
Lighting up the sky for half a second.
Rain pouring and hail spitting down on us.
Swirling wind surrounds us,
Snatching up everything it can.

Shadows close in on us,
Hiding everything.
Until the morning comes,
Battling against the dark,
And succeeding.

Lotte Wakeham (9)

POEM FOR JULIA

There is a girl I care for,
I worship from afar,
She's always in my thoughts,
Her name is Julia.

I can see her strolling,
Through the streets of Tunbridge Wells,
Looking in shop windows,
At all the things they sell.

Going out of an evening,
Having fun at night,
Drinking lots of cider,
Lots of Diamond White.

Lighting up a building,
As she walks into a room,
Laughing rather loudly,
Hope I can see her soon.

I know she's too young,
That is what they say,
Best to give up now,
Maybe another day.

If only I could see her,
Be with her tonight,
I could stop this longing,
And everything would be all right.

Tell her what I'm feeling,
Make this dream come true,
Julia if you're out there,
This poem is for you.

Simon Taylor

A TRUE FRIEND

Someone on whom you depend,
Emotions you cannot pretend,
Loving feelings now descend
The warmth that's given by a friend.

Confidences shared and kept,
Comforting the tears wept,
Sharing dreams that you have slept
And corridors of care you've crept.

Thinking of her tender face,
Picturing her style and grace,
Gentle arms that you embrace
A person you cannot replace.

A true friend.

Sarah Maycock

GODMERSHAM PARK

Set in a valley, south of the city, cradled by downs, alongside the Stour,
Godmersham Park, the dignified home in Regency times of a novelist's
                                                                                      brother.
Georgian style, its two wings make it wide and welcoming, warm red brick,
its open aspect, many windows front and rear allow in light.
A homely house for a favourite aunt loved by children, eleven in all,
a constant visitor, teacher and friend, blessed with sympathy, wisdom
                                                                                       and wit.

In moments of leisure the garden calls the writer to share its beauty quiet;
Wilderness, Temple and shrubbery cool provide her with space and time
                                                                                  to reflect.
Here she could conjure with ideas and thoughts; of heroines Elinor, Emma
                                                                                and Jane,
describe country houses, the Pump Room at Bath, poke fun at the clergy and
                                                                            Lady de Bourgh.
Now her readers praise the knowledge that she shows of humankind,
which she saw and grew to love here in this peaceful Kentish scene.

M Wilson

THE BLUEBELLS ARE GROWING

The bluebells are growing in the slaughtered wood.
The great wind blew here, destroying the trees,
And now the woodmen have come, made fires,
Piled logs, and the smell of wood smoke
Drifts and mingles with the blue flowers.

My steps scrunch the silence; religiously I
Avoid the flowers, the sacrilege of treading them.
The wood becomes a lonely field, the field a great valley
Speckled with farms, lined with roads,
And the silence is pierced by children's shouts.

Gerald Roberts

THE BEACON

A bench, a view, folk in twos,
Sunday walks, paths that fork.
There froths below clouds of green,
Wild cherry, larch, oak and birch bark's sheen.
Amongst them float rare birds that chatter,
Above, prams and feet, roll and clatter,
Three trunks dead, their bellies arch,
Round rocks that cooled these ageing larch.
For roots are dead, and rocks bereaved,
Into the chasm, one strong wind will heave,
Branches screaming, crack and splinter,
For them, no Spring, it will be always Winter.
The beauty of their verdant grave,
Will rejuvenate the growth they crave.
Heed the foaming canopy!
Gossamer blossoms, lacy leaves,
We *know* we owe our lives to trees.
For every breath and subtle hue,
Our spirits lift and thoughts renew.
For Peace is here for all to see,
The best things in life *are* truly free!

Judy Bugg

LIFE ON THE WIGHT

The Isle of Wight is rather small,
With roads that seem to bend.
Don't attempt to drive too fast,
You'll come right off the end.
Our pace of life is very slow,
This saying we all must follow
Never do today,
What you can put off till tomorrow;
Come and see The Needles,
But those you cannot thread.
If not, there's always coloured sands,
At Alum Bay instead.
There's Godshills Model Village,
Or visit Sandown Zoo.
The L A Bowl and Balcony
Lots to see and do.
You'll find the Islanders friendly,
There's such a pretty sight.
Nowhere else I'd rather be,
Than the wonderful Isle of Wight.

A D Beaumont

ST HELENS SHORE

As the wind splits your hair
The shingle hurts your feet -
Seagulls scream
And you feel the heat -
The heat of the earth
The drumbeat of life
Penetrating your body
Bending your shape with its strife.

Waves crashing, ever lashing.
Horses racing, characters chasing,
Collecting shingle, sifting and sorting
Then left to mingle.
You twist and turn
As though to a rhythm
A rhythm of life to which you belong
A rhythm with a song.

Beverley Beck

EARLY CALL

Tangerine ball lifts her head from the mist,
The sea's horizon appears to be kissed
With fiery embers scattered in line -
'Tis my view from the Down, the day's to be fine.

Boson is sniffing the overnight trail
Of a rabbit now hidden; look at his tail
As he darts to and fro with wheels on his feet -
'Tis my scene on the Down, my dog's never *beat*.

The gorse and the shrubs that the frost cannot bite
Burst forth with colour - a beautiful sight.
The dewpond half-full from the overnight rain;
'Tis my path on the Down I'm walking again.

Philip Cook

SANDOWN

The sun begins its descent
Slipping slowly behind rolling green hills.
The cows continue their grazing
Unconcerned with the darkening sky.
The beaches are empty now
Save for the gulls splashing on the ebbing tide?
Ice-cream kiosks stand shuttered against the night
Deckchairs await collection
Striped canvas flapping in the breeze.
Lights go out one by one in the hotels
And curtains shut out the twinkling stars
And Sandown sleeps.

Paula Jacobs

ACROSS THE WATER

This journey 'cross the water
Can be like a dream
Watching other weary travellers
in the haze of warm sunbeams
I see the men out fishing
And the rich man on his yacht
the drone of the ferry's engines
Oh I'm happy with my lot
The Captain's voice breaks my reverie
'Fishbourne, make your way back to your cars'
I drive towards a sunset which
Will soon make way for stars

My eyes take in the landscape of my Island home

This journey 'cross the water
A nightmare is today
I feel my spirits plummet
It always is the way
The fishermen look sullen
Nothing at all feels right
Rich men on yachts perplex me
Because I'm leaving Wight
'We're now approaching Portsmouth'
The Captain's voice does say
I feel now close to panic
We're going the wrong way

My eyes look back in longing at my Island home

Linsey Brown

WOODSIDE BAY

Into Wootton then down a rugged track,
Our old car trundled with me in the back,
Bucket and spade at the ready,
And if he was good I would sometimes take teddy,
This was a great adventure for me,
Packing the house to take to the sea,
At the end of our journey with bags in our hands,
It was a trek thro' a wood to get to the sands,
If we arrived and the tide was out,
Time to see if the cockles were about,
Then on to the rocks where there were winkles galore,
Could any little girl ask for more,
The tide then turns we make a retreat,
For a little rest and something to eat,
An icy reward for being good,
could be bought from the café at the side of the wood,

I remember the big juke box there.

Now back to the beach more time to play,
Whilst Mum, Dad and others in the sun lay.
With my bubbly costume on it's time for a dip,
Across on the Solent goes yet another ship,
Many happy days were spent in this bay,
Laughing and digging my time away.

Mary Grace Jones

PERSEVERANCE

I took a trip to Alum Bay,
To get some coloured sands,
And filled a tube with colours gay,
In horizontal bands.

On reaching home I viewed my prize,
With anger and dismay,
The sand I'd packed so carefully,
Was uniform and gray.

For years with lens and brush I strove,
To grade each tiny grain,
And now at last my task is done,
The tube's sand-striped again!

Albert Hart

ON THE CLIFFS OF ST LAWRENCE

Up, on the hills in the distance the sight of the sea
and everything is quiet as quiet as can be.
Everything so quiet so peaceful and so still
there up, on the grassy silent standing hill.
The flowers just standing happy in the ground
and all is quiet and peaceful, not a sound.
The distant cry of singing birds
And up, on the hill the sheep in herds.
Up, on the hill as silent as can be
and all to watch is the beauty to see.

Chantelle Terry

OUR GREAT WIGHT HOPE

Flotsam and jetsam's graveyards,
On many an upper beach;
What treasures of the world
Are hidden within each :-
Bottles from the Orient,
With messages of love;
Plastic bags from Germany
And a carved Israeli dove;
Coke cans from America;
A wooden box from Spain;
An oar from the rowing club,
Just along the lane;
A china doll from China,
With rather matted hair;
A coconut from Africa
And a rubber Russian bear -
If only humans mingled
Just as peacefully;
How happy all of us,
In this World could be.

Edward Lyon

OUR FUN ISLAND

Holidaymakers happy and free, catch a ferry across the sea.
They come to visit a glorious sight, the place is called The Isle of Wight.
Oh yes the Island beckons folk, in colourful clothes, who laugh and joke.
Off the ferry with suncreamed faces, struggling along with all their cases.
I live here and have to say, I see these visits in a funny old way.
Because you see they do go potty - holidays make most people dotty.
And oh here comes another season - bringing with it all unreason.
It seems that those who cometh hence, leave behind all commonsense.

On first day, sun is hot and phew! Latest arrivals with pink skin - new.
Bare arms, bare all, they all turn red, next day holed up in their bed.
The wonderful bays a great delight, with endless bodies red and white.
The hottest days bring out the most, scattered all along the coast.
Slumped in deckchairs by waterside, hankies on heads and bare feet fried.
Tide then turns, and sea meets feet, with screams, a rush, a quick retreat.
Then on chairlifts, fishing boats, piers and trains and all the various pleasure
planes
They really do not miss a trick, and then they wonder why they're sick!

Cold and blowy still in their shorts, they gather around the main resorts.
Ice cream dripping in their hands, playing ball games on the sands.
Hurricanes can sweep the scene, but still the bikini clad and lean
Lie in heaps between the rocks, amongst their towels, underwear and socks.
There's museums, castles they flock there too! A Queen's lovely home and a
very nice zoo.
Vineyards, theme parks, gardens and farms, cameras click click in hot sweaty
palms.
Walkers ramble along lovely coastal paths, their dress a bit unusual, they often
look really daft.
Knobbly knees, tough boots, already for a trek, and good quality binoculars
hung around their neck.

Then there's cars full of people, and maps galore, they do things they've not done before.
They stop mid roundabout to view 'Hey look at that!' don't mind they queue.
Then winter approaches wasps and swimsuits go, we wait with anticipation for that little bit of snow.
But now coaches soon arrive with the OAPs, but that's another story, *tut,* I really am a tease!
But I really like our visitors have no doubt, even if they're funny when out and about.
In the winter when it's quiet, its great to have it so, but still I'm really sorry when the Holidaymakers go.

Our Island's such a lovely place - its way beyond compare.
A little piece of Heaven - it's something we can share.

Frances M Rapley

ALONE AGAIN

Another day, another night,
The hours pass, slip put of sight.
TV's on, not much to see
It's only there for company.
I wander around, find things to do
But all I want is to talk to you.
I climb the stairs it's time for sleep
But thoughts of you to my mind will creep
The children sleep, I hear them breathe,
They're miles away in make believe.
I look at the clock, it's nearly eleven
And you've been gone since half past seven.
An empty space here in our bed
A pillow smooth that awaits a head.
I've all I need, no reason to moan,
But how I hate this feeling alone.
Somewhere outside a dog is barking,
I hear the sound of a car that's parking,
A key in the door, my heart beat's fast
It's half past twelve and you're home at last.

Kim A'Court

ALL'S NOT ROSY IN THE GARDEN ISLE

It started when aunt May was sick
They came in the dead of night
They wiped out uncle's vegetables
Vile human blight.

Uncle Tom's a widower now
Auntie died last year
Again they came in the dead of night
To fill his life with fear.

While Uncle slept his lonely sleep
Cowards were busy below
For this old man was easy prey
He wouldn't 'have a go'.

His precious greenhouse is no more
They smashed it with their stones
They hurt him more by doing that
Than if they broke his bones.

Christmas came and out they crawled
To violate the weak
They stole Tom's meagre savings
And left his Yuletide bleak.

He doesn't complain or ever moan
Worse happened in the wars
Is it the fate of our elderly
To mutely grieve behind closed doors?

Maureen Matthews

OUR GARDEN ISLE

To spend some pleasant time awhile,
Come visit on our garden isle.
From golden sands and rolling downs
To villages and busy towns.
Bowling greens and skating rinks,
And lovely gardens full of pinks.
From thatched roof cottages and church,
We have it all if you but search.
A forest green with ancient trees,
And yachts a sailing in the breeze.
You'll find we've stately homes galore,
And when you come you'll see much more,
There's nowhere ever quite the same,
And once you've been, you'll come again.

E Maxfield

TRIP TO THE NEEDLES 1994

Cormorants perch silent on the ridges,
In lines of black dots.
Between two rocks, a space
Where long ago a chalk column crashed;
Waves wash over its stump.
At the end of the row the lighthouse stands.
A keeper sits at its base,
Reading a newspaper,
As if in some normal backyard.
Then our boat turns away;
The massive blocks recede,
Becoming distant white stones
On a small postcard.

Julia Perren

THERE IS AN ISLAND

There is an island
Where cares won't find you,
But just remind you
Of when you were free.
A lullaby-land
That's for forgetting.
A sylvan setting
In a silver sea.
Come walk beside an ancient wall,
A forest path, a windy cliff,
A sandy shore
And up a velvet down.
This is our island,
So diamond-like and small, it's
No wonder people call it
The jewel in the crown.

Lawrence Holofcener

ISLAND REFUGE

Chased by the wind, I strode the hills
The verdant downs of limestone Wight,
Below me crashed the billowing waves,
Frothed by the muscular sea-wind's might.

Lashed by the wind, the downland flowers
Lay horizontal on the trembling grasses,
Trees bowed their trunks and shrubs their heads
As subjects when a monarch passes.

Whipped by the wind, my eyes sprang tears,
My clothing seemed as flapping sails,
Breath snatched from lungs, voice drowned in air,
As still the blustering wind assails.

Then one step on, one downward pace
I found a little hillside womb,
A hollow scooped by, who knows what?
A silent, sheltered, windless room.

Contemplative in my peaceful bower
While the shrill wind still rushes overhead,
Into the solitude a thought arose, and spoke,
'This is your still quiet voice,' it said.

Sometimes when life's winds buffet me
And blow as if they'll never cease,
My island refuge comes to calm my soul
And once again I am at peace.

Barry Jones

PORTRAIT OF AN ISLE

A tranquil place or a friendly smile,
Can always be found on a tourist Isle,
Whatever the season,
Let me show you -

Autumn sun glows softly on the mill pond,
Telling us that summer is almost done,
But carnival time is still alive,
Illuminated processions light the sky -

In winter on the shores of Brook,
The sea is wild and angry,
Yet in the wetlands,
The river Yar,
Winds peacefully through the valley -

Spring teases shy blossom to show,
Their wonderful palette of colour,
As bluebells carpet America Wood,
The new-born season awakens all -

Warm golden sand and gentle sea breezes,
Tell us that summer is here,
Children's laughter soars high,
Above the roar of the waves,
Till the sun sinks lower in the sky -

Yet the picture remains unfinished,
Though enchanting and serene,
Like the seasons this Isle is ever-changing,
And loved will always be.

A L Dowden and L T I Dowden

BY THE SEA

Wild sea crashing,
Lashing.
Small boats tipping,
Dipping.
Spray cloud flying,
White gulls crying.
Cold wind blowing,
Tide line showing.
Lonely beach,
Homely beach.

Inside cafe, frothy coffee,
Cigarettes and buns.
Steamed up windows,
Chattering voices.
Coin in slot and
music comes.

I am the sea,
the spray and boat,
Disguised as I am
with umbrella and coat.
Yet needing to stop
along with the crowd,
and the coffee and buns
and music loud.

Liz Pecksen

THE ISLE OF WIGHT

This lovely Isle, surrounded by its restless seas
Where yachts with sails like coloured butterflies,
Skim o'er its surface with such perfect ease.
Where mighty liners sail majestically,
And seabirds dip and wheel in the blue skies
With cries of joy at every balmy breeze
That lifts them high into the clear sweet air.
This Island, with its cliffs that rise
Like Sentinels guarding all that dwell therein.
The forests where the sun glints through the trees.
Where squirrels run, and birds sing melodies to Fox and Badger.
Fields where cattle graze on lush green grass.
The downs which rise along its centre, where men walked
Thousands of years ago, and where now they sleep
In mounds, 'Until the day break'.
Where the huge dinosaurs did roam, and now return, like phantoms of
                                                                         the past.
The little inlets, where the surf, and swell of sea
Invades the beach and then retreats, so wonderfully.
The towns which nestle unobtrusively, which are, for all, a real necessity.
This lovely island, once adored by the great Queen Victoria
Who dwelt here till her dying day.
With all its beauty, all its great delight,
God bless this lovely place, this Isle of Wight.

Joyce Shotter

TIME ON YOUR HANDS

Come on folks, do not despair!
Let us take a walk in the fresh air
Time on your hands, and that means hours
Now you can study birds, trees and flowers
Nature is full of surprises galore
Beautiful butterflies and so much more.

When the weather changes, pause for a while
Someone is needing only your smile
Go to that person and show with giving
You'll make one's life really worth living
Offer your hand in some direction
Although it may be not to perfection
Remember your visit and smile on your face
Is making this world a happier place

June Lane

YAVERLAND

Sleepy little windows wink their tiny eyes
Among their walls of ancient stone on which a thatched roof lies
Around their cobbled borders, standing in array
Is a mass of coloured flowers, a wonderful display
On the hillside near them, a flock of lambs and sheep
Softly doze in still repose, while all the village sleep
The farmer, out so early, walks to check all's well
And the caws of rooks in highest nooks, slowly start to swell
They fly down over duck pond, no occupants to see
But in years gone by, their brother's cry, would welcome you and me
Farther up the only road, the Manor House still stands
Solid, old, big and bold, lord of furrowed lands
Steeped in ancient history, old stories it could tell
Stories of St Urians Copse, and village there as well
The invasion by the Frenchmen, the people that were lost
The pillage and the plunder and the people's total cost
But all this is well hidden, the tourist doesn't see
What's gone on in history, and what you used to be
Although there's church and Manor and the cottages of stone
That secret lies from prying eyes, its yours and yours alone!

C West

HOME

Be it autumn, winter, spring or summer vacation
the Isle of Wight, without exception was the destination.
Then, one day, all my family piled into the car
and somehow, the docks at Portsmouth just didn't seem to be so far.
On reaching there we calmly drove on board the ship
with Cheshire cat grins adorning our faces throughout the trip
for we knew the very next time our feet were to meet dry land
and see the fantastic scenery, the sparkling sea and sifting sand,
that this idyllic place was going to be new life, new home,
where local folk never seemed to let us feel alone
because in an instant there they were as kind as could be,
with introductions, offers of help and cups of tea.
Now we feel we've lived here forever, not just a while
and I can think of no place better to raise my family that this Isle.

Chris Pennell

THE HAVEN

Softly, softly,
Water breaks against the sand,
Its song, a calming tune;
The sky,
An array of vivid colours,
Reflected in the sea,
A glorious sight, saying goodbye,
Slowly it falls,
Disappearing until tomorrow;
A gentle breeze rushes by,
The smell of salt hangs,
The sky darkens,
With it the pale sand cools,
The moon begins to glow,
And the night draws in,
Looking after my haven until tomorrow.

Jane Elgar

MY ISLAND

Oh little island short and wide
With history bulging from side to side,
How do you keep your hills so green
And your cliffs as white as ever I've seen?
A safe retreat for wildlife to home,
Who saw the dinosaurs freely roam,
With soil so rich to grow any stray seed,
On which your plains we richly feed.
And although I've travelled far and wide,
I've always returned to be by your side,
Each time your sides slip my only fear,
Is my dearest island should soon disappear.

Sam Lea

VENTNOR IN SPRING

Ventnor in Spring
Ventnor is a special place
With a charm that's all it's own,
Where in the spring,
If carefully you look,
The shy little violets grow,
Only if you are special too,
With a childlike kindly heart,
Ventnor will show to you her charm,
And grant you inner calm.
The rolling downs on one side,
The other the sparkling sea.
How good is God to give us,
Such perfect tranquillity.

Ivy Barnes

A TRIBUTE TO THE ARCH ROCK

The island's arch Rock was famous,
For ages it withstood wind and rain,
But now, alas it has fallen,
The coastline will not be the same.

To mark the end of this landmark,
An exhibition was duly staged,
Craftwork, poems and photos,
And Joy Johnstone put pen to page.

On the occasion of the opening,
Down there at Freshwater Bay,
Colwell Sunshine club went singing,
To help brighten up the day.

First came the handbell ringers,
Then the intro and speeches few,
The poems by the children,
Were winners through and through.

The singing, you may think I'm biased,
But not from where I stood,
Those standing round about me,
Thought they were very good.

The island MP, attended,
He was glad to be in West Wight,
The hotels chef, made a 'Rock Cake',
This 'Arch Rock' looked a great sight.

The exhibition is long over,
All the displays now packed away,
But the *Famous Arch Rock* is not forgotten,
By the folk of Freshwater Bay.

Will A Tilyard

ST CATHERINE'S DOWN

The final stage, when tackled from the west,
is steep - the climb, with pharos, rocket-shaped
and penance-built, as goal, worth-while;
for there a modern Moses, one surveys
a promised land - beholds, eight-hundred feet
below, its widespread features: Channel: chines;
a forest; farms with chequered pasture-lands
which merge in far-off hills - observes the glint
of weathercock refulgent in the sun,
or sees the coastal sandstone yield to chalk
that rising sheer adds drama to the view -
on tranquil days an ideal rendezvous.
But should a midnight mission take one there
when gale-force winds whip cloud-wrack over moon,
rebuff the climber, and with baleful sound
evoke the ghosts of long-forgotten monks;
transformed, the milieu loses its appeal -
the bracken hides the adder, and the night
conceals arcana steeped in time.

T C Hudson

MY HEAVEN

As a child I knew of heaven.
   A blue sky,
Underneath my mother, my father and I
Sat on a hillside among green, sweet grass,
The sun was radiant in her beauty
and tingled on my skin.
My childhood is over, but still
My vision remains,
Its heaven I'm in.

Lois Prior

THE LONGSTONE

Battered by wind, rain and snow,
For centuries I'm a place to come and go.
While viper and lizard play cat and mouse,
The Woodpecker laughs near the great old house.
Standing tall amongst the growth of spring,
Where Blackcap, Willow Warbler and Chiffchaff sing.
The glisten in a foxes eye, the soaring Buzzard pass me by,
Through fern and campion young rabbits play.
A sinking sun ends another day.
No cuckoo calls on a moonlit night,
But a Nightjar makes its silhouette flight.
A Badger snorts the cool night air
A Barn owl's screech, a Barn owl's stare.
Next time you travellers go passing by.
Are you watched by the Longstone or a Kestrel's eye.

Nigel Cantelo

ODE TO 2 MISCARRIED CHILDREN

You twinkled brightly in your parent's eyes
So lightly like 2 fragile butterflies
And then were lost in an unworldly haze of pain
Never to see sunlight, snow or rain.

The nurses were kind and comforted us
'One in five pregnancies ends thus'
You were so innocent and not to know
To us your deaths were a crushing blow
Why? we asked again and again
Unable to dredge an answer from the doctor's (or my) brain

Time heals all wounds as time goes by
But first we'll have a little cry
For two unborn babes in the womb
Who, in death, were granted no blissful tomb.

Derek Barretto

THE VIEW OF A HILLINGDON HOUSEWIFE

We've trains, shops and buses in good supply.
Streets are busy, traffic emissions high.
Planes from Northolt and Heathrow fly our skies.
Mount Vernon, Harefield, hospitals nearby.

Sirens tell of accidents and crime,
it's good to know they can reach us in time.
The Citadel but half an hour away.
On the train we'll go there to spend the day.

Woodland, canals, rivers, lakes we can see.
For bird watchers, walkers, bliss you'll agree.
These green belt spaces free for all to share,
give tranquillity if you've time to spare.

We live in a semi with neighbours around,
small gardens, parking places thin on the ground.
We've centres for hobbies. Theatres? We've three
This Hillingdon is quite a good place for me.

Wendy Edwards

THE HEART OF LONDON

Hand to me a star, and I will show you whence,
Lies a city that glitters more, and fills you with a sense.
A sense that carries you forth, on wings of timeless days.
Of a bounty more fully, which beneath the streets there lays.
You can feel it as you walk, and hear it in the wind.
You can see it as it flies, swift through the sky; as a Hawk.
It lets you feel a part, and yet lets you feel alone;
As it weaves its magic around, and makes itself be known.
Forever more you'll find, your life you will share,
For when you stroll through London, its heart beats everywhere.

Eve Schmidt

NON OLD LONDON

brown fog of old
engulfed now by new decades shining
of glass offices
turning grimy institutions
into tall reflections
towering over London Bridge

in an air static
with extremes
day switches on night
night switches off day
the Thames turns South Bank lights
into salubrious pulses

in this city of moving sights
realities rush towards realities
history sits upon history
as if time is waiting to guard itself
against perpetuity

and the new reality - another generation
flowing at an unreal pace
in a city rich with relics
of its own modernity

with coming and going
or act of remaining
until they happen
as all the exciting
and/or frightening
tiring changes

Lewis Breakspear

YOUNG CLERGY ON RETREAT

On a hot, planted afternoon
Reclining in convent air,
Distant sisters
Weeding, calling to cat,
Sincere voices
Bowl
Unsuspecting God.

Held tight, spat on,
Polished and shiny,
Mystery hurling with intent
Towards gripped defending gestures.
Sincere voices
Batting
Weakened God.

And under running feet
Ground softens on
Thick roots of faith;
Ugly, twisted, uncomfortable in light.
Overhead,
Sincere voices
Are cheering
Vanishing God.

Mark Oakley

WAR AND PEACE IN THE NINETIES

So much competition in this world,
The Serbs against the Croats,
The IRA up against Britain,
Just as if it is a big games
A deadly game for innocent children

Iraq wanted Kuwait's land and oil.
War started, UN sent troops
With stormin' Norman leading in victory.
Not just winning but loss is felt,
Both sides lose life, so precious, so long.

Then the wars in the same streets.
Bitchy young females with attitude problems,
Mouthy youths who have to prove themselves,
Gangs, against different race and religion,
Negative, malicious, hopeless: life in the nineties.

Some people don't care and I'm not
Ashamed to admit it: I can't care
Anymore, too much trouble, and I
Have too little sympathy. I am not alone.
This, this, fiasco is life in the nineties.

Leah Carpenter

THE HIGH HORSE HAS A RIDER STILL

With hatred technicoloured and all human frailty,
Newsprint stinks of filth and blood,
Goodwill is blacklisted into obscurity;
Where's the good? What's the good?
It's not too late, it's not too late.
The high horse has a rider still.

Though hearths look listless and low,
And thinking is dimmed by half-light,
Stars will shine and rivers will flow;
Who needs a candle in the sun's light?
The high horse has a rider still

It will pass - this winter of malcontent,
Two sparrows will fetch fivepence,
And the swallow will pay his rent,
Real values will return with Spring's good sense.
The high horse has a rider still.

Mary Frances Mooney

I LEARN TO SPEAK

Speechless. I was, silently speechless;
Spasmodically, sporadically speechless.
Suddenly, somebody started to sorrowfully see,
Soon as I picked up my pen, opened my mouth and
Started to speak.

Charlette de Christi

LONDON 1995

London's streets,
Paved with gold?
Or clogged with traffic,
Exhausting us all.

Heavy pollution,
Choking our air.
Cannot breathe,
Getting nowhere.

Felling the trees,
That once street-lined
Communities shattered,
By youthful crime

What future for London?
It's looking bleak.
What a shame politicians,
Only plan ahead a week.

Sheila Atherton

LONDON

London, my London, where I was born
Where I first drew breath and saw the dawn
Where the Thames flowed fast and the Tower stood bold
Where first I beheld the knights of old
Clad in their armour so fierce and grey
In the White Tower, not the king's highway;
Where the traffic honks, the buses stop and start
To pick up people from stops way apart;
Where the roads are busy with hundreds intent
On sightseeing and shopping for presents well meant.
For the tired and weary with aching feet,
Regents Park offers a welcome retreat
From the noise and bustle of Oxford Street.
There the trees spread their shade, the flowers their perfume
And you can listen to the band play *Claire de Lune.*
London, where there is so much to do
The cinema, theatre or paintings to view
Where galleries, museums and libraries too
Are all there ready to interest you;
Where you can sit on a seat in nearby Kew
And watch the boats pass in front of you;
Where cricket is watched by enthusiastic crowds
And cheering and clapping sometimes abounds.
Where whatever your mood there is something to see
So London, my London, is the place for me.

Doris Sherman

LONDON, MUCH MALIGNED

London, much maligned,
environmentally unfriendly,
called 'the smoke' by the carping north.
Only Londoners know its worth.

Yes, London's bells resolutely ring
even though nightingales no longer sing
in Berkley Square.

At dead of night
poets look out from garrets above the turrets
to breathe fresh air from Hampstead Heath.
Old moon smiles on jostling roofs beneath
and late revellers break the silence
of an empty street.

The capital's landscape cannot sleep.
Houses lean together, whispering
secrets they don't mean to keep.
Curtains hide casements concealing the whole
and the infinite windows of London's soul.

Peggy Trott

GOLDERS HILL PARK

Am I in Africa
Where animals screech
And call
To their neighbours
On the open plain
Where the
Sky is dipped
In swimming dark
Blue ink
And silver pools
Of light
As the
Grass stands stiff
Bleached to white
Like straw
As the bark
Suited trees
Move gently with
The whisper
Of a breathless
Breeze
Am I in a perfect
Dream
As other couples
Romantically roam
Towards the rung bell
And the city below
As we head out
Of the park
Towards home.

Miriam Eissa

TIME ON MY HANDS

The gold watch ticks to a strict rhythm,
Taking twenty five years, it is comfortable on my wrist.
How hard to come to terms with not having a routine.
Strolling along Fleet Street, there are echoes in my mind.
Sunday sun shines through the clouds,
Gleaming on one side of the street, unable to penetrate to the other.
How contrasting is this morning!
Doors firmly shut, just the noise of the nearby traffic.
The occasional London taxi passes by, but it is still and peaceful.
Lincoln's Inn Fields is now inviting me to come in to reflect on my life.
With pigeons for company, they eagerly await their food.
Haunting are the memories of achievements through dedication.
The dome of St Pauls rises magnificently in front of me as I continue
                                                                my journey.
Majestically, it dominates the city skyline.
It, too, is resting from the fumes of the exhausts.
With the offices reaching for the sky, advancement is here to stay.
As I turn around for one last time,
I contemplate my new life.
The view of the Underground sign is welcoming.
The gold watch informs me that my duty has been completed.

Shirley D Press

POEM ON THE LONDON UNDERGROUND

Doors (on the train) close and open
open and close.

Someone must know something
but nobody speaks.

Travelling tongue-tied.
Journeying lips that do not move.

There are many shoes available for scrutiny on the underground.

And yes!
The occasional poem

startling in its truth
leaps out

so silently.

You would hardly notice it was there
next to the advertisements.

Jean Beith

LONDON

London has so many faces;
        bustling streets with many races
        quiet lakes and leafy trees;
        man can work, or take his ease.
        Pageantry from ages past;
        great cathedrals built to last.

Palace royal and squalid slum;
        near or far the traffic's hum;
        noble stores where doormen stand;
        where the wealthy in our land
        clothe themselves expensively;
        go to Fortnum's for their tea.

Suburbs rich and suburbs poor;
        dossers sleeping on the floor;
        barrow-boys on corners yell
        trying doubtful wares to sell;
        jewellery, a watch or two
        till a 'bobby' hoves in view.

All existence can be seen
        on a bus to Golders Green.
        Or, if time cannot be found
        speed on London's Underground.
        See the jewels in The Tower;
        visit Kew in summer flower.

Hub of commerce . . . quiet retreat . . .
        parks with grass for weary feet . . .
Ancient . . . modern . . . proud and free!
        London is the world to me.

Marjorie W Bedford

IN LOVING MEMORY OF A CAT

The flat seems quiet, and empty now,
A stillness will prevail.
Sometimes, I think I hear you meow,
Or see you flick your tail.

I'll reach the door, to let you in,
To find - there's no-one there,
And miss the feel of your velvety chin,
As you'd jump on the back of my chair.

I rise each morning from my bed,
And feel the need to hurry,
My Pusskin's waiting to be fed -
Then know, I need not worry.

I'll miss the little trill you made,
As though to say 'Hello',
When creeping 'neath my counterpane,
Where you knew you should not go.

You'd run ahead, along the hall,
Tail high, and tummy swaying,
Then from the kitchen, start to call,
'Where's tea mum?' you'd be saying.

No more, your chilly little nose,
Will rub against my ear.
I hope you'll have a sweet repose,
My precious little dear.

Hilda Jones

BAD NEWS

The news is very bad today, but then it always is,
With someone committing murder or raping little kids.
There's dire news in the papers, and on television too
Its enough to make one wonder, what this world is coming to
We lock our doors and windows, before we go to bed
And daren't send kids on errands
In case they end up dead.
Surely there is someone who can put these things right
And stop all the muggings, the stealing and the fights,
If we used the brains God gave us for good instead of ill,
Then maybe we could do it, with lots of goodwill,
For its brother against brother,
Nations against other lands
It needs someone very great
To make us all hold hands.
All hold hands together to banish sin and strife
We should all join with God to make a better life,
With a good future for our children
And care for old folks too
With care and faith and fortitude
I'm sure we could see things through
For faith in God is what we need,
To get us through with pride,
Then we will get our just rewards,
When we reach that other side.

C Holmes

UNTITLED

There is no harm so cruel as that born of innocence.
A child creating flame to discover its beauty
A woman creating life unwanted through the simple probings of curiosity
Most of all, a love created or destroyed by ignorance of life
A crime, a judge, and a jury, innocence, conscience, and indulgence
But can there be no verdict?

John Spiller

GRADE 1 LISTED BUILDING

Set out to paint a picture
What subject should it be?
A little bit of London
For you and me to see.

He walked along the Serpentine
Strolled around Hyde Park
Then he sketched 'The magazine'
Before it got too dark

Years later payed a visit
To good old *Sotherby's*
Took the little picture
What value could it be?

The picture now takes pride of place
Hung upon a wall
Gives a lot of pleasure
Not to one but all

It's all thanks to God
'The magazine' restored
A little piece of history
There to be adored.

E Hyder

THE BLUE AND WHITE BRIDGE

As the arms reach across
The river
In an effort to join hands,
I know that someone
Wants to join the strands.
The image of the statue
Is powerfully
Moving,
Bringing together a
City torn in two.

Nearby, the blue and white
Bridge
Links land and land.

I've heard afresh
Stories seen on TV
Years ago,
From people who
Really know the words that
'A divided city cannot
Stand'.

And Lonndonderry City
Waits for the reality
Of the image
In the statue.

Nearby, the blue and white
Bridge
Links land and land.

Pauline Long

FOREIGN GLASS

The bottom of the glass
Lays empty in my hand
Drunk in hazy bar room
In a foreign land
On the ship I travelled
Just to get away
From a life as dismal
As a British day
Humdrums of the nine to five
Is severed from my brain
Rainy days on Mondays
Eroded them away
Homeless nights on the streets
Are far away from me
In the bar room
That I sit
As hazy as can be.

Graham Hagger

TELL ME THE TRUTH ABOUT LONDON

'Tell me the truth about London' -
What do you want to hear?
Tales of spiral staircases, flowers, breakfast dawns in French brasseries
Foggy streets pierced by lonely headlights
Power drills and plaster of Paris
The dust - the heat - car fumes - elevator music
Beggars and sailors, street women and junkies
Strangers on trains and drunks in the alley
Policemen and thieves and travelling salesmen
Mansions and ghettos, graveyards and playgrounds
People in boxes of cardboard and concrete
London -
      Fantastic and bold
      Faceless and boring
A god on the streets, a face in the crowd
And the way the sun beats down
Is how I feel inside.

David A H Clark

THE ENIGMA OF LONDON

What is it about London, my parents came from here,
though fate decreed a Yorkshireman was the brand
that I should bear

Yet that same hand eventually drew me back to this
our town, the one place that belongs to all, the
jewel in our crown.

To know this town is to enjoy such feelings of love
and hate, but what else in a place so complex and
yet so desolate.

This city of beauty, antiquity and wealth, side by
side with poverty and shame, oh! what will rid us
of this dreadful pain.

In adversity our city stands so proud, but in times
of peace seems somewhat bowed, entertainment for all
yet one is lonely in the crowd.

Some would never seek to roam and can only think of
London as their home, whilst others tossed on stormy
sea struggle helplessly to flee.

Can anywhere so vast and great be able to accommodate
the needs of all who gather there and not leave many
in deep despair.

Will this Enigma ever be understood, will there ever be
only sunshine in the wood, where glades of beauty and
joy abound for all in this our London town.

B S Ashwell

THE SEA

Hark! Listen to the sea
pounding on the shore, never
ending its moving evermore.
        The tides changeth.
        The sea comes in.
        The sea goes out.
We don't know what it's all about
At night you can hear it,
Pounding against the shore,
Making the moonlight dazzle
even more.
Sounding familiar, the waves
Crash to and fro, making
Splashing noises we soon get used
to know. Fascination takes
over us, listening to the sea.
Wondering what secrets it
keeps from you and me.

Margaret Brown

RESTORATION OF WESTBURY WHITE HORSE

The horse was carved on Bratton hill
In Alfred's time, to mark his victory -
Through many years it proudly stood there still,
Placed high above for near and far to see.

Then, sad to say, by time and weather's wearing,
The whiteness dulled, the figure shone no more.
Till now, after long months of work and caring,
We see it clearly as it was of yore -
In all its former glory re-appearing
There stands again a white 'White Horse' once more.

Rosemary Smith

FLOWERS FOR YOU

I only pluck a flower or two
And they are the one's I give to you
You thought your garden was yours forever,
Not thinking of time, and whatever

Your garden grew so strong and well,
No one knew, no-one could tell,
That soon you would live alone,
No-one to toil the soil you own,

But thinking of your garden past,
Bring memories that always last.
Pleasure comes now, when you smile,
And dream of your garden, for just a while.

Enjoy these flowers I plucked for you,
For one day, I may be like you too.

Carol Shaikh

BIRTHDAYS

The postman brings our cards to the door
We open them up.
We're enthralled by them all.
The verses we read
mean such a lot, our
friends and relations they
haven't forgot, to send
a card on our special
day. Another year gone
by. You'll hear people
say, Candles on the
cake we light. It
fills our day with
such delight.

Margaret Brown

ETERNAL SPRING

When winter's dark
It's shroud so bold
Sears the byre and the hurdled fold
Then rustles and whistles and with low pitched moans
By day and night in winter's tones.

Now no autumnal stars do shine their light
Now only the cold whispering winds of night
In different motions await the hour
Fur and feather in nature's power.

Little thrushes sung their song
Little robins lie cold and gone
Grim is nature's frugal hand
So sparse their diet on all the land.

But soon the verdant eternal spring
Will spread its aura as if on wings
And mites of blossom will soon appear
Near wayside places and far and near.

And then good summer days will come around
And the cuck'o will call across the down
And the swallows will come
With their circulating flights
On some summer evening before the night.

D E Porter

BEHIND THE HEDGES

They'll write about the great white horses.
Cathedrals, abbeys village churches.
Fine tributes will be paid to monuments
and names. This county's treasures
are diverse.

But for me the heart of Wiltshire's here
Sitting close to Muriel in Arthur's
special chair

Looking out from timbered gables
onto lawns with wooden tables.
Rockeries and paths and roses,
Scents of honesty and peace.

Unmarred by all the tests of time -
farm and home and garden
All tucked up behind the hedges
in a place called.

Brokers Wood

ON MARLBOROUGH DOWNS

We took the steep gaily, Tassie and me,
We passed the Five Alls and the old bakery -
Proof that a lot of life's best things are free,
If you've ever smelled hot bread and lardie!
I bent to the bar of her little pushcart,
Smiled into the rosy face dear to my heart;
My heels were too high, but were *ever* so smart!
I was twenty-one, happy and hardy.
So come up, my lovie, where friends often meet
On Calvert's broad steps at the end of the street
Then, the town at our back, there'll be Goldenlands wheat
And the downs, where the lambs will be leaping.
Clickety-tap went my shoes on the road
As I sped past the green and each ancient abode,
With my little push-chair and its lovable load,
(Her blue eyes under bonnet-brim peeping).
Now high on the downs, under vasty blue skies,
I laughed at my little one's crow of surprise
As the first early swallows with jubilant cries
Swooped over us, dipping and skimming.
Look, Tassie! Look there! See the dear lambs at play?
And that ribbon of silver below, far away?
That's our little Kennet. Remember that day,
Stoneybridges? The water-rat swimming?
Then away went the shoes with the elegant heels,
The push-chair stood still, on its wobbly wheels,
The wind took her bonnet, her rapturous squeals
As we ran, as we rolled, in the grasses.
You can still take that walk and see much the same view,
I believe it's as green, and the sky's wide and blue.
But, that day on the downs, in the year '52,
That was ours. It was mine, it was Tassie's.

Kay Boorman

INFORMATION

We hope you have enjoyed reading this book - and that you will continue to enjoy it in the coming years.

If you like reading and writing poetry drop us a line, or give us a call, and we'll send you a free information pack.

>Anchor Books Information
>1-2 Wainman Road
>Woodston
>Peterborough
>PE2 7BU